·→ ‖ ACKNOWLEDGEMENTS ‖ ←·

The publishers would like to thank the following sources for permission to reproduce their pictures:

FINE ART PHOTOGRAPHS & LIBRARY LTD: pages 11, 13, 14, 17, 25, 29, 30, 41, 43, 46, 55, 56, 59, 65, 66, 72, 79, 80, 85, 86, 93, 96, 100, 102, 105, 108, 113, 114, 116, 119, 121, 122, 125

E.T. ARCHIVE: pages 18, 21, 23, 35, 38, 48, 49, 68, 88, 91, 94, 111

THE BRIDGEMAN ART LIBRARY: pages 45, 76, 99, 106

THE CHRIS BEETLES GALLERY, LONDON: pages 8, 22, 26, 36, 51, 52, 60, 71, 75, 110

THE MARY EVANS PICTURE LIBRARY: pages 10, 64

The publishers would also like to acknowledge the following writers and poets:

p.8 THOMAS LOVELL BEDDOES (1803-1849) *Song, Torrismond*
p.9 W. SOMERSET MAUGHAM (1874-1965) *The Summing Up*
p.10 ELIZABETH TOLLET (1694-1754) *Winter Song*
p.12 WILLIAM SHAKESPEARE (1564-1616)
p.13 ALICE WALKER (b.1944)
p.15 THOMAS PAINE (1737-1809)
p.16 ANTOINE DE SAINT-EXUPÉRY (1900-1944) *The Little Prince*
p.18 JOHN DRYDEN (1631-1700) *Secret-Love or The Maiden Queen*
p.19 HELEN KELLER (1880-1968)
p.20 EDMUND WALLER (1608-1687) *Go Lovely Rose*
p.22 JOHN CLARE (1793-1864) *First Love*
p.23 JUAN RUIZ DE ALARCÓN MENDOZA (c.1283-c.1350) *El Amor*
p.25 THOMAS CAMPBELL (1777-1844)
p.26 WILLIAM WORDSWORTH (1770-1850)
p.27 MAXIM GORKY (1868-1936) *The Zykovs*
p.31 SIR PHILIP SIDNEY (1554-1586) *The Bargain*
p.33 ROBERT HERRICK (1591-1674) *The Shoe Tying*
p.34 PAUL GÉRALDY (b.1885) *l'Homme et l'Amour*
p.36 RABINDRANATH TAGORE (1861-1941) *Fruit Gathering*
p.37 WILLIAM SHAKESPEARE (1564-1616) *As You Like It*
p.39 DECIMUS JUNIUS JUVENAL SATIRES (c.60-140 A.D.)
p.41 JOHN KEBLE (1792-1866) *The Christian Year*
p.43 ROBERT HERRICK (1591-1674) *The Primrose*
p.44 SAMUEL TAYLOR COLERIDGE (1772-1834)
p.45 THOMAS CAREW (1598-1638) *Celia Singing*
p.46 WILLIAM WORDSWORTH (1770-1850) *She was a Phantom of Delight*
p.47 SAMUEL BUTLER (1612-80)
p.49 LAWRENCE HOPE (1865-1904) *Carpe Diem*
p.50 GEOFFREY CHAUCER (1340-1400) *The Romaunt of the Rose*
p.53 PERCY BYSSHE SHELLEY (1792-1822)
p.55 WILLIAM CAVENDISH (1592-1676) *Love Play*

p.56 ROBERT BROWNING (1812-1889) *You'll Love Me Yet*
p.57 ROBERT BURNS (1759-1796) *O my Love is like a Red, Red Rose*
p.58 JOHN KEATS (1795-1821) *A Thing of Beauty from "Endymion"*
p.61 THOMAS OTWAY (1652-1685) *Captive*
p.62 WILLIAM SHAKESPEARE (1564-1616) *A Midsummer Night's Dream*
p.63 KAHLIL GIBRAN (1883-1931)
p.64 THOMAS LOVELL BEDDOES (1803-1849) *The Reason Why*
p.66 WILLIAM SHAKESPEARE (1564-1616) *Sonnet*
p.67 JOHANN WOLFGANG GOETHE (1749-1832) *Elective Affinities*
p.69 THOMAS CAMPION (1567-1620) *Never Love*
p.71 WILLIAM BLAKE (1757-1827) *Love's Secret*
p.73 JAPANESE LYRIC
p.74 HENRY WADSWORTH LONGFELLOW (1807-1882)
p.76 PERCY BYSSHE SHELLEY (1792-1822) *Love's Philosophy*
p.77 MARK TWAIN (1835-1910)
p.78 ALGERNON SWINBURNE (1837-1909)
p.81 ANON *To His Love*
p.82 CHRISTINA ROSSETTI (1830-1894) *Echo*
p.83 JOHN FREEMAN (1880-1929) *Nearness*
p.84 ARTHUR SYMONS (1865-1945) *Memory*
p.86 ALFRED EDWARD HOUSMAN (1859-1936) *Tell Me Not Here*
p.87 WILLIAM BLAKE (1757-1827)
p.89 EMILY DICKINSON (1830-1886) *Love Poems*
p.91 ANNE MORROW LINDBERGH (b.1906) *Second Sowing*
p.92 JOHN DRYDEN (1631-1700) *Amphitryon*
p.95 SARAH WILLIAMS (1841-68) *The Offering of the Heart*
p.96 THOMAS WOLFE (1900-1938) *Of Time and the River*
p.97 CHRISTINA ROSSETTI (1830-1894) *Remember*
p.98 THOMAS MOORE (1779-1852) *The Silent Voice*
p.101 RAINER MARIA RILKE (1875-1926) *Letters to a Young Poet*
p.102 NATHANIAL HAWTHORNE (1804-1864) *American Note-Books*
p.104 WILLIAM WORDSWORTH (1770-1850) *Why Art Thou Silent*
p.106 GEORGE GORDON BYRON (1788-1824) *She Walks in Beauty*
p.107 WILLIAM BLAKE (1757-1827) *The Smile*
p.109 STENDHAL (1783-1842) *On Love*
p.110 SIR WALTER SCOTT (1771-1832) *The Lay of the Last Minstrel*
p.113 JACQUES MARITAIN (1882-1973)
p.115 RABINDRANATH TAGORE (1861-1941) *Fruit Gathering*
p.116 JOHN KEATS (1795-1821) *In a Drear-Nighted December*
p.118 EDGAR ALLAN POE (1809-1849) *To One in Paradise*
p.121 WYSTAN HUGH AUDEN (1907-1973) *Notes on the Comic, The Dyer's Hand*
p.123 JOHN DRYDEN (1621-1700) *Ah, How Sweet it is to Love*
p.124 BLAISE PASCAL (1623-62)

THE LOVERS' BOOK OF DAYS

Designed and produced by THE BRIDGEWATER BOOK CO. LTD

Compiled by Rhoda Nottridge

Edited by Joanne Jessop

Designed by Peter Bridgewater

Picture Research by Felicity Cox

Typesetting by Vanessa Good/Chris Lanaway

Published by
CHARTWELL BOOKS, INC.
A Division of **BOOK SALES, INC.**
110 Enterprise Avenue
Secaucus, New Jersey 07094
CLB 3229
This edition published in 1994
© 1993 CLB Publishing, Godalming, Surrey, England
All rights reserved
Printed in Italy
ISBN 0-7858-0086-7

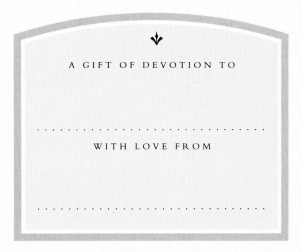

A GIFT OF DEVOTION TO

. . . .

WITH LOVE FROM

. . . .

CHARTWELL
BOOKS, INC.

THE LOVERS'

❧ BOOK OF DAYS ❧

A Romantic Book of Days for Lovers everywhere

THE LOVERS'

JANUARY

How many times do I love thee dear?
Tell me how many thoughts there be
In the atmosphere
Of a new-fall'n year,
Whose white and sable hours appear
The latest flake of Eternity:
So many times do I love thee, dear.

THOMAS LOVELL

BEDDOES

JANUARY

1

2

3

4

5

6

7

NOTES

We are not the same persons this year as last; nor are those we love. It is a happy chance if we, changing, continue to love a changed person.

W. SOMERSET MAUGHAM

LEFT: *Girl in a White and Gold Headscarf,* EDWARD TAYLOR (1828-1906)

JANUARY

Ask me no more, my
truth to prove,
What I would suffer for my love.
With thee I would in exile go
To regions of eternal snow,
O'er floods by solid ice confined,
Through forest bare with
northern wind . . .

ELIZABETH TOLLET

8

9

10

11

12

13

14

NOTES

A Love Duet, FREDERICK WILLIAM HAYES (1848–1918)

15

16

17

18

ST AGNES' EVE

St Agnes is the protector of virgins and was put to death for refusing to marry a man she did not love. On St Agnes' Eve, a girl can divine who her husband will be by baking a 'dumb' cake.

Make a mixture of eggs, flour, water and salt into a cake, remaining dumb and fasting during the preparation. Mark with your initials and put the cake on the coals of a fire, to cook slowly through the night, first reciting:

Sweet St Agnes, work thy fast
If ever I be to marry man,
Or ever man to marry me
I hope him this night to see.

At midnight the spirit of the girl's future partner will turn the cake for her and prick his initials on it next to hers.

_____

_19_

_____

_20_

_____

_21_

_____

NOTES

_____

I have learned not to worry about love; but to honor its coming with all my heart.

ALICE WALKER

Feeding the Birds, VINCENTA DE PARADES (1870-1910)

The Gallant Skater, FREDERICK HENDRICK KAEMMERER (1839–1902)

JANUARY

22

23

24

25

26

27

28

NOTES

'Tis that delightsome transport
  we can feel
Which painters cannot paint,
Nor words reveal,
Nor any art we know
  of can conceal.

THOMAS PAINE

JANUARY

If you tame me, then we shall need each other. To me, you will be unique in all the world. To you, I shall be unique in all the world.

ANTOINE DE
SAINT-EXUPÉRY

29

30

31

NOTES

NOTES

NOTES

NOTES

NOTES

The Bridal Sleigh Leaving a Snowbound Village, ALFRED VON WIERUSZ KOWALSKI (1849–1915)

THE
LOVERS'
FEBRUARY

I feed a flame within, which so torments me
That it both pains my heart, and
yet contents me:
'Tis such a pleasing smart, and I so love it,
That I had rather die than once remove it.
Yet he for whom I grieve shall
never know it;
My tongue does not betray, nor
my eyes show it.
Not a sigh, nor a tear, my pain discloses,
But they fall silently, like dew on roses.

JOHN DRYDEN

FEBRUARY

1

2

3

4

5

6

7

NOTES

The best and most beautiful things in the world cannot be seen or even touched. They must be felt with the heart.

HELEN KELLER

LEFT: *The Kiss*, FRANCESCO HAYEZ (1791–1881)

FEBRUARY

Go lovely Rose

Tell her that wastes her

 time and me,

That now she knows

When I resemble her to thee

How sweet she seems to be . . .

EDMUND WALLER

8

9

10

11

12

13

14

NOTES

King Rene's Honeymoon, DANTE GABRIEL ROSSETTI (1828–1882)

FEBRUARY

I never saw so sweet a face
As that I stood before:
My heart has left its
dwelling-place
And can return no more.

JOHN CLARE

15

16

17

18

19

20

21

NOTES

Love makes a subtle man out of a crude one, it gives eloquence to the mute, it gives courage to the cowardly and makes the idle quick and sharp.

JUAN RUIZ

Lady and Prince Wrapped in Quilt, INDIAN PAINTING (c1800)

Hearts Are Trumps, GEORGE EDWIN KILBURNE (1839-1924)

FEBRUARY

_____ 22 _____

_____ 23 _____

_____ 24 _____

_____ 25 _____

_____ 26 _____

_____ 27 _____

_____ 28 _____

_____ 29 _____

_____   _____

THE
LOVERS'

·»‖ MARCH ‖«·

It is the first mild day of March
Each minute sweeter than before,
The redbreast sings from the tall larch
That stands beside our door.
There is a blessing in the air,
Which seems a sense of joy to yield
To the bare trees, and mountains bare,
And grass in the green field.
Love, now a universal birth,
From heart to heart is stealing,
From earth to man, from man to earth:
It is the hour of feeling.

WILLIAM WORDSWORTH

MARCH

1

2

3

4

5

6

When one loves somebody,
everything is clear - where to go,
what to do - it all takes care of
itself and one doesn't have to ask
anybody about anything.

MAXIM GORKY

7

NOTES

LEFT: *By The Sea*, CHARLES GREEN (1840-1898)

MARCH

8

9

10

11

12

13

14

NOTES

A Romantic Interlude, HENRY ANDREWS (1830–1860)

The Gamekeeper's Courtship, GEORGE BERNARD O'NEILL (1828–1917)

MARCH

15

16

17

18

19

20

21

NOTES

My true love hath my heart,
and I have his,
By just exchange one for
another given:
I hold his dear, and mine he
cannot miss,
There never was a better
bargain driven:
My true love hath my heart,
and I have his.

SIR PHILIP SIDNEY

MARCH

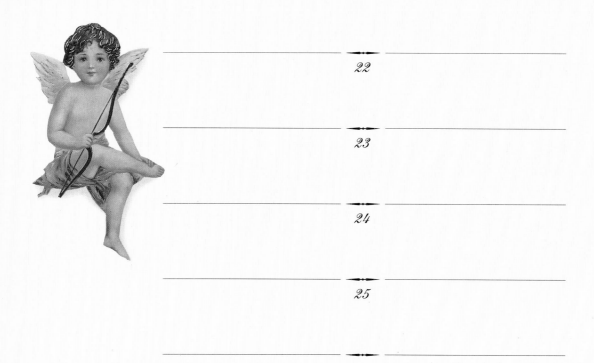

22

23

24

25

26

27

28

NOTES

THE VIOLET OF VENUS

The great lover Napoleon adopted the tiny violet as the emblem of his Imperial
Napoleonic Party. If picked in the last quarter of the moon, these tiny blooms are
said to have love-provoking powers. To make your love still sweeter, prepare a
violet sorbet by mixing together the following:

1 white of egg
2 tablespoons of lime juice
300ml/1 cup of grape juice
50g/2oz caster sugar/superfine sugar
200ml/½ cup sugar syrup
4 tablespoons of crème de
  violette

Put the egg white and caster sugar to one side, mix the rest of the ingredients together and freeze until mushy. Then beat the egg white and fold in the caster sugar. Add all the mixture together and freeze. Serve topped with a few fresh violet flowers.

MARCH

29

30

31

NOTES

NOTES

NOTES

NOTES

NOTES

We must resemble each other a little in order to understand each other, but we must be a little different to love each other.

PAUL GÉRALDY

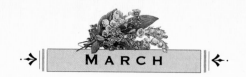

Psyche Carried off by Zephyr, EGISTO FERRONI (1835–1912)

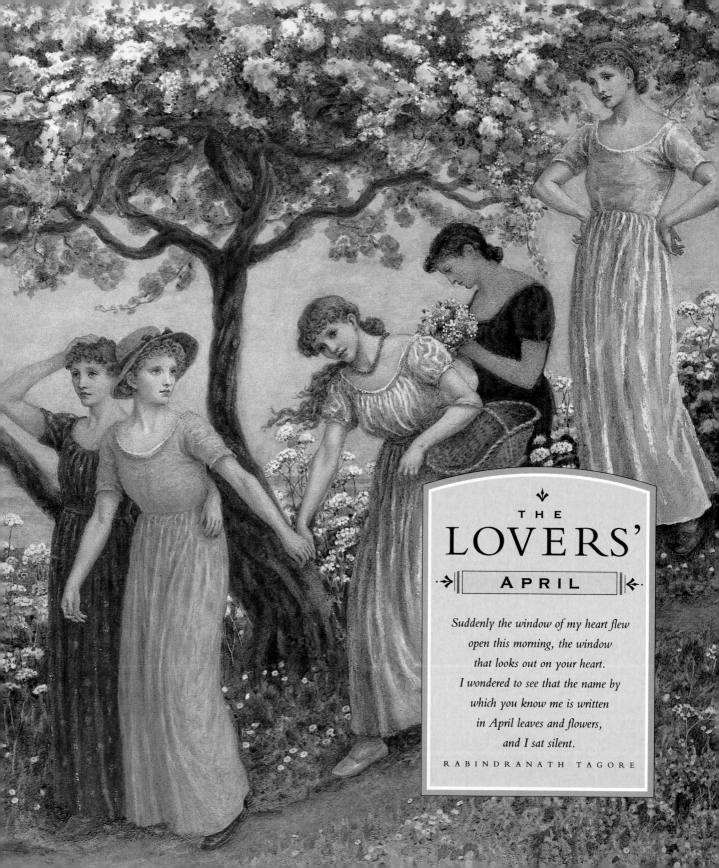

THE LOVERS' APRIL

Suddenly the window of my heart flew
open this morning, the window
that looks out on your heart.
I wondered to see that the name by
which you know me is written
in April leaves and flowers,
and I sat silent.

RABINDRANATH TAGORE

APRIL

1

2

3

4

5

6

7

NOTES

*If thou remember'st
not the slightest folly
That ever love did make
thee run into,
Thou hast not loved.*

WILLIAM
SHAKESPEARE

LEFT: *Through the White Flowers,* KATE GREENAWAY (1846–1901)

Lover Telling of Love to Lady, CHRISTINE DE PISIAN (Mid 15th Century)

APRIL

8

9

10

11

12

13

14

NOTES

Nature, in giving tears to man, confessed that he Had a tender heart; this is our noblest quality.

DECIMUS JUNIUS JUVENAL

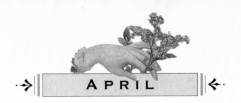

APRIL

15

16

17

18

19

20

21

NOTES

Sweet is the smile of home;
the mutual look,
When hearts are of each
other sure.

JOHN KEBLE

A Pensive Mood, CHARLES SILLEM LIDDERDALE (1831–1895)

APRIL

22

23

24

25

A LOVER'S SPELL

To enhance love, this spell can be done by two lovers together.

Cut twelve hearts out of deep red-colored paper. Write your lover's name on six of the hearts and at the same time ask your lover to write his or her name on the other six.

Lay down a small mirror face up and put the hearts around it, alternating the name of your lover with your own. Light a red candle to rekindle passion and look down into the mirror, repeating your lover's name six times. Each time you do this, pick up one of the hearts with your lover's name on.

Take it in turns to sew one of the hearts to another with red thread. When all the hearts are sewn together, put them in a place where you want your love together to thrive.

APRIL

———— 26 ————

———— 27 ————

———— 28 ————

NOTES

————

Ask me why I send you here
This sweet infanta of the year?
Ask me why I send to you
This primrose, thus bepearl'd
with dew?
I will whisper to your ears:
The sweets of love are mix'd
with tears.

ROBERT HERRICK

APRIL

*If I had but two little wings
And were a little
feathery bird,
To you I'd fly, my dear!
But thoughts like these are
idle things,
And I stay here*

SAMUEL TAYLOR
COLERIDGE

29

30

NOTES

NOTES

NOTES

NOTES

NOTES

NOTES

You that think Love
* can convey No other way*
But through the eyes,
* into the heart, His fatal dart,*
Close up those casements,
* and but hear This syren sing;*
And on the wing
Of her sweet voice it
* shall appear*
That Love can enter
through the ear.

THOMAS CAREW

A Man and a Woman at a Casement, FRA FILIPPO LIPPI (1406–1469)

THE
LOVERS'
MAY

She was a phantom of delight
When first she gleamed upon my sight;
A lovely apparition sent
To be a moment's ornament;
Her eyes as stars of twilight fair;
Like twilight's, too, her dusky hair;
But all things else about her drawn
From May-time and the cheerful dawn;
A dancing shape, an image gay,
To haunt, to startle, and waylay.

WILLIAM WORDSWORTH

MAY

_____ 1 _____

_____ 2 _____

_____ 3 _____

_____ 4 _____

_____ 5 _____

_____ 6 _____

_____ 7 _____

NOTES

*All love at first, like
generous wine,
Ferments and frets, until
'tis fine . . .*
SAMUEL BUTLER

LEFT: *Gathering Wild Flowers*, ALFRED GLENDENING (JNR) (1861–1907)

MAY

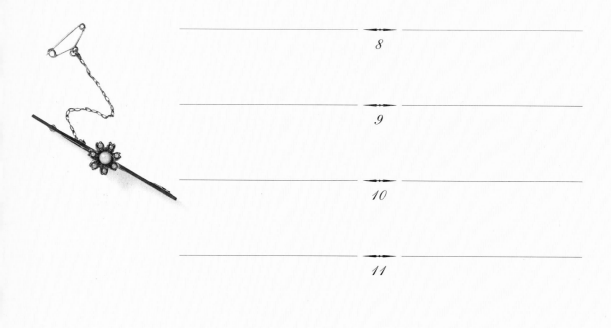

—————————————————————— ❖ ——————————————————————

8

—————————————————————— ❖ ——————————————————————

9

—————————————————————— ❖ ——————————————————————

10

—————————————————————— ❖ ——————————————————————

11

—————————————————————— ❖ ——————————————————————

DAISY

INNOCENCE

MAY

12

13

14

NOTES

And if Fate remember later, and
  come to claim her due,
What sorrow will be greater than
  the Joy I had with you?
For today, lit by your laughter,
  between the crushing years,
I will chance, in the hereafter,
  eternities of tears.

LAWRENCE HOPE

MAY

> *Hard is the heart that loveth nought in May.*
>
> GEOFFREY CHAUCER

15

16

17

18

19

20

21

NOTES

Reading a Book, EDWARD TAYLER (1828–1906)

By the Window, JOHN SIMMONS (FL.1850)

MAY

_____

22

_____

23

_____

24

_____

25

_____

26

_____

27

_____

28

_____

NOTES

_____

Familiar acts are beautiful
through love.

PERCY BYSSHE SHELLEY

MAY

29

30

31

N O T E S

N O T E S

N O T E S

N O T E S

N O T E S

Sweet, let us love enjoy,
And play and tick and toy,
And all our cares will drown;
Smile, laugh, and
    sometimes frown,
Make love's parenthesis
With a sweet, melting kiss.

WILLIAM CAVENDISH

Alain Chartier, EDMUND BLAIR LEIGHTON (1903–1922)

THE
LOVERS'

JUNE

You'll love me yet! and I can tarry
Your love's protracted growing:
June reared that bunch of
flowers you carry,
From seeds of April's sowing.

ROBERT BROWNING

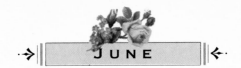

JUNE

O my Luve's like a
red, red rose,
That's newly sprung in June;
O my Luve's like the melodie
That's sweetly play'd
in tune.

ROBERT BURNS

1

2

3

4

5

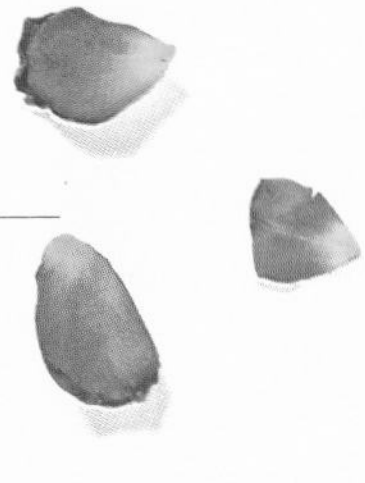

6

7

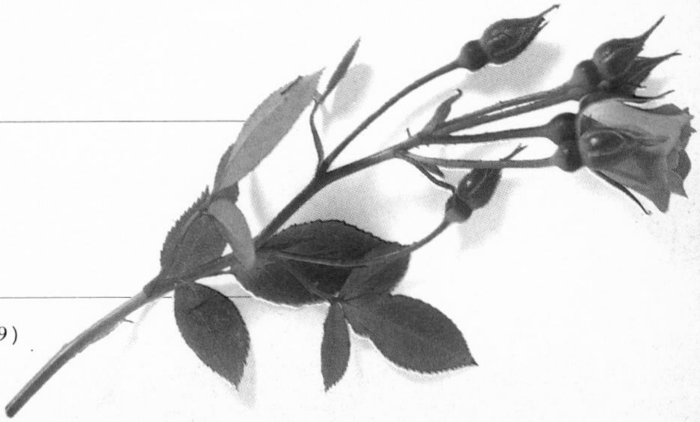

NOTES

LEFT: *A Secret Admirer*, PIERRE OUTIN (1840-1899)

_____
_____ ◆ _____

8

_____
_____ ◆ _____

A thing of beauty is a
  joy for ever:
Its loveliness increases; it
  will never
Pass into nothingness; but
  still will keep
A bower quiet for us,
  and a sleep
Full of sweet dreams, and
  health, and quiet breathing . . .

JOHN KEATS

9

_____
_____ ◆ _____

10

_____
_____ ◆ _____

11

_____
_____ ◆ _____

12

_____
_____ ◆ _____

13

_____
_____ ◆ _____

14

_____
_____ ◆ _____

NOTES

_____
_____ ◆ _____

Sweethearts, FREDERICK MORGAN (1856-1927)

Fete Champetre, JOHN MASEY WRIGHT OWS (1777-1866)

JUNE

_____ ◆ _____
15

_____ ◆ _____
16

_____ ◆ _____
17

_____ ◆ _____
18

_____ ◆ _____
19

_____ ◆ _____
20

_____ ◆ _____
21

_____ ◆ _____
NOTES

_____ ◆ _____

I did but look and
love awhile,
'Twas but for one half-hour;
Then to resist I had no will,
And now I have no power.

THOMAS OTWAY

JUNE

22

23

24

25

THE PRETTY PANSY

The pretty pansy was said to have been painted purple by one of cupid's arrows. As a bringer of kind thoughts and love, it is also called heart's ease; an infusion of pansy petals will cure a broken-hearted lover of all pain. Puck mischievously used an infusion of pansies to create chaos in A Midsummer Night's Dream:

Yet markt I where the bolt of
  Cupid fell:
It fell upon a little western flower.
Before milk-white, now purple
  with love's wound,
And maidens call it love-in-idleness.

Fetch me that flower; the herb I
  shew'd thee once:
The juice of it on sleeping eyelids laid
Will make man or woman madly dote
Upon the next live creature
  that it sees.

WILLIAM SHAKESPEARE

JUNE

———— ❧ ————
26

———— ❧ ————
27

———— ❧ ————
28

———— ❧ ————
NOTES

———— ❧ ————

*Love has no other desire
but to fulfil itself. To melt and to
be like a running brook that
sings its melody to the night.
To wake at dawn with a winged
heart and give thanks for another
day of loving.*

KAHLIL GIBRAN

JUNE

I love thee and I love thee not,
I love thee, yet I'd rather not,
All of thee, yet I know
not what . . .

THOMAS LOVELL
BEDDOES

—————————— ❖ ——————————
29

—————————— ❖ ——————————
30

—————————— ❖ ——————————
NOTES

—————————— ❖ ——————————
NOTES

—————————— ❖ ——————————
NOTES

—————————— ❖ ——————————
NOTES

—————————— ❖ ——————————
NOTES

—————————— ❖ ——————————
NOTES

—————————— ◆ ——————————

Reflection, Herman Jean Joseph Richir (1866–1942)

THE LOVERS'

JULY

Shall I compare thee to a summer's day?
Thou art more lovely and more temperate:
Rough winds do shake the
darling buds of May,
And summer's lease hath all
too short a date:
Sometime too hot the eye
of heaven shines,
And often is his gold complexion dimm'd;
And every fair from fair
sometimes declines,
By chance, or nature's changing
course, untrimm'd;
But thy eternal summer shall not fade . . .

WILLIAM SHAKESPEARE

JULY

→| J U L Y |←

———— 1 ————

———— 2 ————

———— 3 ————

———— 4 ————

A life without love, without the presence of the beloved, is nothing but a mere magic-lantern show. We draw out slide after slide, swiftly tiring of each, and pushing it back to make haste for the next.

JOHANN WOLFGANG GOETHE

———— 5 ————

———— 6 ————

———— 7 ————

NOTES

LEFT: *The Flirtatious Fisherman*, EDWIN THOMAS ROBERTS (1840–1917)

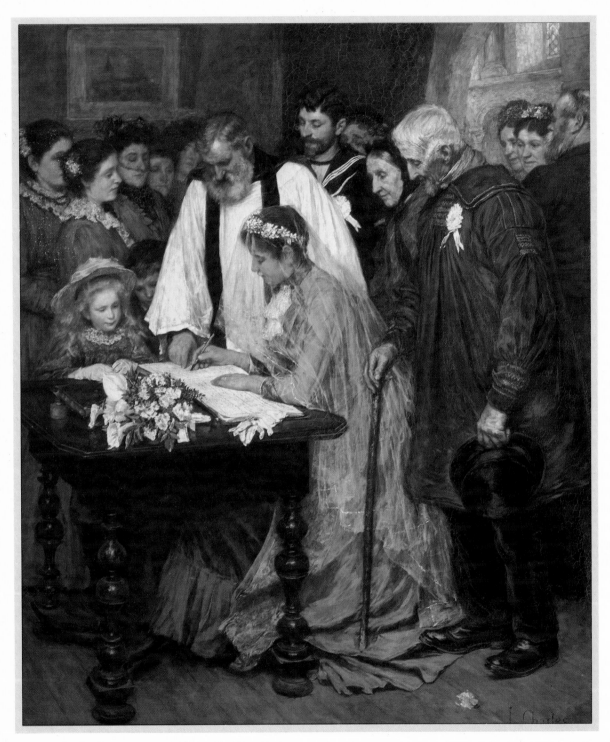

Signing the Register, JAMES CHARLES (1851–1906)

JULY

8

9

10

11

12

13

14

NOTES

Never love unless you can
Bear with all the faults of man:
Men will sometimes jealous be,
Though but little cause they see;
And hang the head, as discontent
And speak what straight they
  will repent.

THOMAS CAMPION

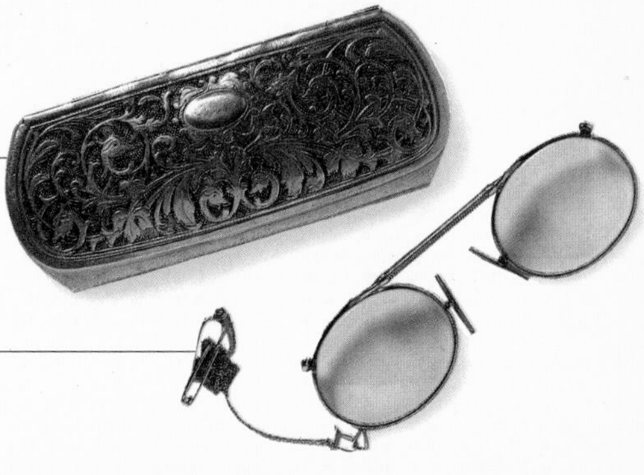

JULY

15

16

17

18

DRUID'S DRAUGHT

*In the heat of the summer, try sipping a refreshing Druid draught of immortality.
Take no more than a silver tablespoonful of this powerful love potion at sunset
and sunrise for seven days.*

Make an infusion of heather, honeysuckle, red clover and vervain steeped in around 1 cup of pure spring water. Strain the mixture carefully before sipping.

Vervain is one of the Druids' seven sacred herbs, often called upon by witches and magicians to aid seduction plans and act as a cunning aphrodisiac.

JULY

_____

19

_____

20

_____

21

_____

22

_____

Never seek to tell thy love,
Love that never told can be;
For the gentle wind doth move
Silently, invisibly.
I told my love, I told my love,
I told her all my heart,
Trembling, cold in ghastly fears.
All! She did depart!
A traveller came by,
Silently, invisibly:
He took her with a sigh.

WILLIAM BLAKE

On a Riverbank, CHARLES JAMES LEWIS (1830-1892)

JULY

22

23

24

25

26

27

28

NOTES

Two things cannot alter,
Since time was, nor today
The flowing of water;
And love's strange, sweet way.

JAPANESE LYRIC

JULY

29

30

31

NOTES

NOTES

NOTES

NOTES

NOTES

> *Be still, sad heart and*
> *cease repining;*
> *Behind the clouds is the sun*
> *still shining;*
> *Thy fate is the common*
> *fate of all,*
> *Into each life some rain*
> *must fall.*
>
> HENRY WADSWORTH
> LONGFELLOW

The Rose Bearer, EDWARD KILLINGWORTH JOHNSON (1825–1923)

THE
LOVERS'
AUGUST

The fountains mingle with the river
And the rivers with the ocean,
The winds of heaven mix for ever
With a sweet emotion;
Nothing in the world is single;
All things by a law divine
In one spirit meet and mingle
Why not I with thine?

PERCY BYSSHE SHELLEY

————— ◆ —————
1

————— ◆ —————
2

————— ◆ —————
3

————— ◆ —————
4

————— ◆ —————
5

————— ◆ —————
6

————— ◆ —————
7

————— ◆ —————
NOTES

To get the full value of joy,
you must have someone to
divide it with.

MARK TWAIN

————— ◆ —————

LEFT: *The Lover Surprised,* F J SCHALL (1752–1825)

8

9

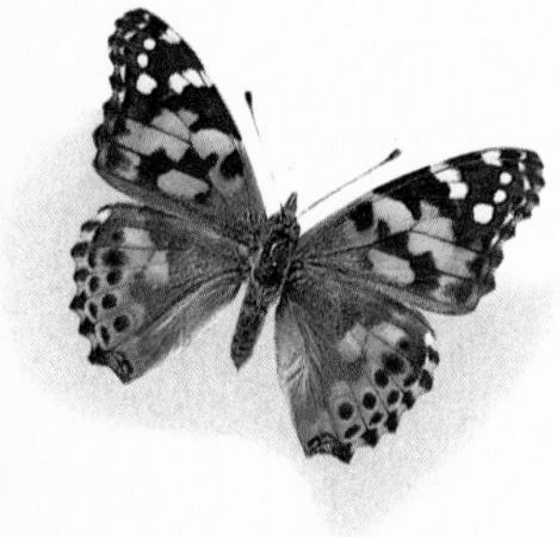

10

11

12

13

14

NOTES

Love, as told by the
seers of old,
Comes as a butterfly tipped
with gold,
Flutters and flies in
sunlit skies,
Weaving round hearts that
were one time cold.

ALGERNON
SWINBURNE

Girl with a Butterfly, HAROLD PIFFARD (1868-1939)

Unfrequented Ways, WILLIAM HENRY GORE (1880-1920)

AUGUST

15

16

17

18

19

20

21

NOTES

Come away! Come sweet Love!
The golden morning wastes,
While the sun, from his sphere,
His fiery arrows casts,
Making all the shadows fly,
Playing, staying, in the grove
To entertain the stealth of love.
Thither, sweet Love, let us hie,
Flying, dying, in desire,
Winged with sweet hopes and
heavenly fire.

ANON

22

23

24

25

THE FAIRY FLOWER

The honeysuckle is said to be a flower of the fairies, its intoxicating scent strongest at nightfall.

A young man could encourage a girl to dream passionately about him by repeating his name three times over a posy made of honeysuckle. He then had to steal into her room, in order to place the posy near her bed, so that as she slept she would breathe in the heady scent.

Come to me in the silence of
the night;
Come in the speaking silence
of a dream;
Come with soft rounded cheeks
and eyes as bright
As sunlight on a stream . . .

CHRISTINA ROSSETTI

AUGUST

26

27

28

NOTES

As perfume doth remain
In the folds where it hath lain,
So the thought of you, remaining
Deeply folded in my brain,
Will not leave me:
all things leave me:
You remain.

ARTHUR SYMONS

29

30

31

NOTES

NOTES

NOTES

NOTES

NOTES

Leisure Moments, ERNEST WALBOURN (1897–1920)

THE
LOVERS'
►◄ SEPTEMBER ►◄

Tell me not here, it needs not saying,
What tune the enchantress plays
In aftermaths of soft September
Or under blanching mays,
For she and I were long acquainted
And I knew all her ways.
On russet floors, by waters idle,
The pine lets fall its cone;
The cuckoo shouts all day at nothing
In leafy dells alone;
And traveller's joy beguiles in autumn
Hearts that have lost their own.

ALFRED EDWARD

HOUSMAN

SEPTEMBER

1

2

3

4

5

6

7

NOTES

Love seeketh not itself to please
Nor for itself hath any care,
But for another gives its ease,
And builds a heaven in
hell's despair.

WILLIAM BLAKE

LEFT: *Love's Letter Box*, ARTHUR HOPKINS (1848–1930)

The Alarm, JEAN FRANCOIS DETROY (1679–1752)

SEPTEMBER

8

9

10

11

12

13

14

> *What fortitude the soul*
> *contains,*
> *That it can so endure,*
> *The accent of a coming foot,*
> *The opening of a door!*
> EMILY DICKINSON

NOTES

SEPTEMBER

15

16

17

18

A WINGED RETURN

A straying lover could be brought back to the straight and narrow by using a gypsy spell. A woman wanting a man to return first had to find the winged seeds of an ash and an oak branch with an acorn. In the myths of some lands the ash tree actually created the first man on earth, so it is a powerful tree to use for calling love. This charm should then be repeated three nights in a row, while the ash and oak are tucked under the woman's pillow:

Acorn cup and ashen key,
Bid my true love come to me -
Between moonlight and firelight,
Bring him over the hills tonight;
Over the meadows, over the moor,
Over the rivers, over the sea,
Over the threshold and in
  at the door.
Acorn cup and ashen key,
Bring my true love back to me.

SEPTEMBER

_19_

_20_

_21_

NOTES

The Lovers, SILVESTRO LEGA (1826–1895)

SEPTEMBER

*Love reckons hours for
months, and days for years;
And every little absence
is an age.*

JOHN DRYDEN

22

23

24

25

26

27

28

NOTES

The Love Letter, GEORGE BERNARD O'NEILL (1828-1917)

Lovers, SZINYEI MERSE PAL (1879)

SEPTEMBER

29

30

NOTES

NOTES

NOTES

NOTES

NOTES

NOTES

Like mine own dear harp is
this my heart
Dumb, without the hand that
sweeps its strings;
Though the hand be careless
or be cruel,
When it comes, my heart breaks
forth and sings.

SARAH WILLIAMS

THE
LOVERS'
❖
⊷ OCTOBER ⊶

*All things on earth point home in old
October: sailors to sea, travelers to walls
and fences, hunters to field and hollow
and the long voice of the hounds, the lover
to the love he has forsaken.*

THOMAS WOLFE

OCTOBER

1

2

3

4

5

6

7

NOTES

*Remember me when I am
gone away,
Gone far away into the
silent land;
When you can no more hold me
by the hand,
Nor I half turn to go, yet
turning stay,
Remember me when no more,
day by day,
You tell me of our future that
you plann'd:
Only remember me: you
understand
It will be too late to counsel
then or pray.*

CHRISTINA ROSSETTI

LEFT: *Absence Makes the Heart Grow Fonder,* MARCUS STONE (1840–1921)

OCTOBER

8

9

10

Love hath a language of
his own -
A voice that goes
From heart to heart - whose
mystic tone
Love only knows.

THOMAS MOORE

11

12

13

14

NOTES

The Orchard, NELLY ERICHSEN (FL.1882–1897)

The Lovers, CESARE AUGUSTIN DETTI (1847–1914)

OCTOBER

15

16

17

18

19

20

21

NOTES

For one human being to love another; that is perhaps the most difficult of all our tasks, the ultimate, the last test and proof, the work for which all other work is but preparation.

RAINER MARIA RILKE

OCTOBER

There is no season when such pleasant and sunny spots may be lighted on, and produce so pleasant an effect on the feelings, as now in October.

NATHANIEL
HAWTHORNE

22

23

24

25

A Rustic Courtship, THOMAS JAMES LLOYD (1849-1910)

26

27

28

NOTES

HALLOWEEN HAZELS

*The supernatural powers of the magic hazel tree are called on in many games
to test a lover's intentions.*

An engaged couple would select a hazelnut each and put them in the fire. If they jumped together in the heat their union would be successful but if one nut jumped out of the fire, that meant the owner would be unfaithful.
For a girl to find out if someone she admired shared her love, she would name the man, place the nut in the fire and demand:
If you love me, pop and fly
If you hate me, burn and die.
A nut that popped loudly, bursting, meant that the man was bursting with love for her, while a nut that did nothing meant there was no interest.

OCTOBER

Why are thou silent! Is thy
love a plant
Of such weak fibre that the
treacherous air
Of absence withers what was
once so fair?

WILLIAM
WORDSWORTH

29

30

31

NOTES

NOTES

NOTES

NOTES

NOTES

OCTOBER

Faraway Thoughts, ANON

THE LOVERS'
→ NOVEMBER ←

She walks in beauty, like the night
Of cloudless climes and starry skies;
And all that's best of dark and bright
Meet in her aspect and her eyes:
Thus mellow'd to that tender light
Which heaven to gaudy day denies.

GEORGE GORDON
BYRON

NOVEMBER

1

2

3

4

5

6

7

NOTES

There is a smile of love,
And there is a smile of deceit,
And there is a smile of smiles
In which these two smiles meet.

WILLIAM BLAKE

LEFT: *The Garden of Eden,* HUGH GOLDWYN RIVIERE (1869-1947)

The Introduction, George Goodwin Kilburne (1839-1924)

NOVEMBER

_8_

_9_

_10_

_11_

_12_

_13_

_14_

*To be loved at first sight, a man
should have at the same time
something to respect and
something to pity in his face.*

STENDHAL

NOTES

NOVEMBER

15

16

17

Love rules the court, the
camp, the grove,
And men below, and
saints above;
For love is heaven, and
heaven is love.

SIR WALTER SCOTT

18

19

20

21

NOTES

Soldier's Farewell, RICHARD COLLINSON (1832–1890)

NOVEMBER

22

23

24

25

APPLE OF MY EYE

The apple has been considered an aphrodisiac ever since Eve tempted
Adam with it in the Garden of Eden. It is the sacred symbol of
love and protection in witchcraft. The juice of apples can be drunk to
attract love or improve prowess.

If an unmarried girl peels an apple in a continuous strip without
breaking it, she should then fling it over her left shoulder. If it falls
in one piece, the shape will indicate the initial of the man.

26

27

28

NOTES

We don't love qualities,
we love a person; sometimes by
reason of their defects as well as
their qualities.

JACQUES MARITAIN

The Tryst, WILLIAM HOLYDAKE (1834–1894)

Knostrop Old Hall, JOHN ATKINSON GRIMSHAW (1836–1893)

NOVEMBER

29

30

NOTES

NOTES

NOTES

NOTES

NOTES

NOTES

The night is dark and your slumber is deep in the hush of my being. Wake, O Pain of Love, for I know not how to open the door, and I stand outside.

RABINDRANATH
TAGORE

THE LOVERS'

►DECEMBER◄

In a drear-nighted December,
Too happy, happy brook,
Thy bubblings ne'er remember
Apollo's summer look;
But with a sweet forgetting,
They stay their crystal fretting,
Never, never petting
About the frozen time.
Ah! would 'twere so with many
A gentle girl and boy!
But were there ever any
Writh'd not at passed joy?
The feel of not to feel it,
When none there is to heal it,
Nor numbed sense to steel it,
Was never said in rhyme.

JOHN KEATS

DECEMBER

—— 1 ——

—— 2 ——

—— 3 ——

—— 4 ——

—— 5 ——

—— 6 ——

—— 7 ——

NOTES

LEFT: *Madame Se Chauffe*, JOHN CALLCOTT HORSLEY (1817-1903)

DECEMBER

Now all my days are trances,
And all my nightly dreams
Are where thy gray
eye glances,
And where thy footstep
gleams -
In what ethereal dances
By what eternal streams!

EDGAR ALLAN POE

8

9

10

11

12

13

14

NOTES

Under the Mistletoe, Edward Frederick Brewtnall (1846–1902)

DECEMBER

15

16

17

18

DECEMBER DELIGHT

The red rose is said to have a blush that came from the blood of
Aphrodite. While attempting to save her lover Adonis, from a wild boar,
she had to clamber through a white bush of briar roses. The blood from
the scratches on her feet stained the briar and gave the world the first
red roses. The red rose has been a lover's symbol ever since.

If a young girl wraps a red rose carefully in white tissue paper on
Midsummer's eve, she should put it away until Christmas.
If on Christmas day she finds it is still intact, she should wear it and
the first man to admire it will become her husband.

DECEMBER

19

20

21

NOTES

Among those whom I like or admire, I can find no common denominator, but among those whom I love, I can: all of them make me laugh.

WYSTAN HUGH AUDEN

Going to a Christmas Party,
GEORGE SHERIDAN KNOWLES (1863-1931)

Christmas Shopping, HAROLD PIFFARD (1895-1899)

DECEMBER

———— ❦ ————
22

———— ❦ ————
23

———— ❦ ————
24

———— ❦ ————
25

———— ❦ ————
26

———— ❦ ————
27

———— ❦ ————
28

———— ❦ ————
NOTES

———— ❦ ————

Love and Time with
 reverence use,
Treat them like a parting friend;
Nor the golden gifts refuse
Which in youth sincere
 they send:
For each year their price is more,
And less simple than before.

JOHN DRYDEN

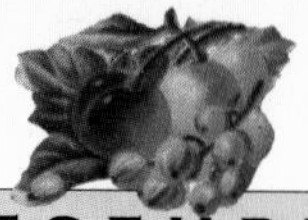

DECEMBER

The heart has its reasons which reason cannot know.

BLAISE PASCAL

29

30

31

NOTES

NOTES

NOTES

NOTES

NOTES

'Twas Ever So, Lovers' Vows Traced in Snow, WILLIAM HOLYDAKE (1834-1894)